Nathaniel Hawthorne   Poems

Nathaniel Hawthorne

POEMS

Edited by Richard E. Peck

Introduction   In his poem "Hawthorne," read before the Phi Beta
Kappa Society at Harvard in 1877, E. C. Stedman said
that, though "prose like his was poesy's high tone,
No carol Hawthorne sang." Stedman was both right and
wrong. One commonly finds descriptions of
Hawthorne as a poet in prose because of his powers
of imagination and the suggestiveness of his fiction.
R. H. Stoddard wrote, "lacking the accomplishments
of verse, [Hawthorne] was in the highest sense a poet."
And James Russell Lowell remembered Hawthorne
as "the greatest poet, though he wrote in prose...that
America has given to the world."

Hawthorne wrote more verse than is commonly
known. The men quoted above should not be criticized
for blindness, however; subsequent generations have
repeated the same opinions. Perhaps this slim book may
redress the balance. Stedman was not above correcting
himself: his *American Anthology 1797-1899* prints
a Hawthorne poem.

Hawthorne never claimed the rank of poet, and even
denied on different occasions that he enjoyed or
often read verse. Yet remarks creep into his prose which
display familiarity with much poetry and many poets.
Even his letters offer comments like the flowery
compliment to Sophia Peabody in December 1839:

> Dearest, I wish your husband had the gift
> of making rhymes; for methinks there
> is poetry in his head and heart, since he has
> been in love with you. You are a Poem, my
> Dove. Of what sort, then? Epic?–mercy on
> me,–no! A sonnet?–no; for that is too
> labored and artificial. My Dove is a sort of
> sweet, simple, gay, pathetic ballad.

Here Hawthorne comes near describing the sort of poems he had already written and was to write: no epics, no sonnets, only slight ballads or—later in his life—limericks.

He probably wrote more verse than is included here. But, regarding his poems lightly, he took no care to preserve them. What verse we do have has come to us through accidental preservation in letters and journals or in the reminiscences of friends more concerned with commemorating Hawthorne the prose stylist.

Four lines of unpublished juvenile verse in the C. Waller Barrett Collection of the University of Virginia's Alderman Library set a trail that led to Salem and Boston newspapers, to Christmas gift annuals, periodicals, letters and journals, and to the holdings of several American libraries. Other poems from Hawthorne's hand may still lie hidden in attics or in private collections, waiting to be flushed from cover.

Yet even this collection, brief though it is, constitutes an addition to the Hawthorne canon interesting beyond its worth as novelty. Many of the poems are less than effective; most predate Hawthorne's college days at Bowdoin. Yet all are intriguing for a number of reasons: a few are thematically related to one another; some are evidence of Hawthorne's youthful, satiric response to currently popular newspaper verse; others demonstrate concerns which found better expression in his fiction; and all provide material for a biographer or for anyone who would see a complete picture of Hawthorne the artist.

Hawthorne's interest in versifying seems to have

flowered early. The first surviving example was written when he was but twelve years old. From that point until he entered Bowdoin College in 1821, he composed most of the other poems included here. The greatest number appeared in a hand-lettered "newspaper" titled "The Spectator," which he circulated among his friends in the Autumn of 1820.

Also in 1820, according to his sister Elizabeth, he tried to place his verse in local newspapers and it was in the Salem *Gazette* that he first saw his literary efforts published, so far as scholars can now tell. Most bibliographies list the novel *Fanshawe* (1828) as his first publication. Predating that novel by nearly three years, "The Ocean" appeared in the *Gazette* on August 26, 1825. It is therefore of particular interest to bibliographers. And, when grouped with the other poems which treat death and the sea or darkness, it may provide yet another clue for the biographer or psychoanalytically inclined critic. His father, Captain Hathorne, failed to return from a voyage to Surinam in 1808, when Hawthorne was but four years old. Like the early pirate stories which his sister tells us Hawthorne burned, the poem deals with the sea, one of his lifelong loves. These poems also offer an answer to those who find the friendship between Hawthorne and Melville an unlikely one. While Melville discussed with Hawthorne his craft as a writer, what did Hawthorne seek from their conversation? Both prose writers wrote verse, but they also shared a love for the sea, and Hawthorne's earliest writing reveals this fondness.

Following the years at Bowdoin and his commitment

to a career as a writer, Hawthorne wrote few poems which survive. Edward Walcott, the "class poet" at Harley College in *Fanshawe*, extemporizes sixteen lines of a drinking song in a scene almost certainly auto-biographical. At Bowdoin, Hawthorne had helped to found the Pot-8-Oh Club at whose functions each member had to recite his own verse. Longfellow, among others, praised Hawthorne's Latin translations and English verse which he saw and heard there.

Surviving examples of verse from the period during which Hawthorne busied himself with his fiction are more rare, though some do remain. Faith Egerton's song in the short story "The Three-Fold Destiny" has seldom been reprinted with that story since its original appearance in the *American Monthly Magazine* (March, 1838).

A few years later, in 1845, two religious poems appeared under Hawthorne's name in a Christmas gift annual, *Scenes in the Life of the Saviour*, edited by Rufus Griswold. The poems, "Walking on the Sea" and "The Star of Calvary," have been admitted to the Hawthorne canon by some and excluded by others. But it does not seem likely that the name, Hawthorne, could mean anyone other than Nathaniel Hawthorne to a reader in 1845. The absence of the first name seems to demonstrate rather than to deny his authorship.

Except, then, for these few poems, Hawthorne seems to have lost, during his final year at Bowdoin, the desire to write poetry. The remaining examples are limericks or, in one case, a gently satiric description of his neighbor, Bronson Alcott, the transcendentalist who founded his own version of the Brook Farm community. Alcott lectured at Fruitlands on his pet theories, among them his vegetarian principles and a reluctance to eat foods other than those which grow upwards, the fruits of the earth which, as he said, aspire to heaven. He is characterized as the "airy sage of Apple Slump."

This gentle jibe at Alcott displays a genial good humor and playfulness which distinguishes Hawthorne's verse from most of his fiction. Even the youthful poems in "The Spectator" are only half-serious imitations of currently popular newspaper verse; they also parody such fare. Hawthorne's poetry shows us a side of the man more often than not neglected.

All this is not to praise Hawthorne's verse in an absolute way. As juvenilia, most of it, of course, lacks the merit of mature work. Yet even the later verse suggests Hawthorne's wisdom in choosing to write in prose and to ignore whatever attraction the poetic muse may once have held for him. Whatever their final shortcomings, the poems reveal a familiarity with metrical patterns, with popular themes, and with poetic diction common to the verse of Hawthorne's contemporaries. Longfellow's juvenilia, for example, can stand little close analysis.

Nevertheless, any literary work of a major artist possesses intrinsic merit not measured by absolute standards. As an artist grows and matures, his tastes and standards change. It is as unwise to judge him solely by his masterwork as it is to ignore his apprenticeship. Both tell us something about the man.

Because many of the poems exist in printed versions only, or in copies by Hawthorne's friends, it is impossible to recover exactly the text of each poem as it came from the author's hand. The aim has been to provide clarity and readability rather than a catalog of every variant reading. The poems are offered in the form of the manuscript where possible but in that of the printed text when that is the only source. Obvious mistakes have been silently corrected and occasional punctuation inserted.

Most of the titles have been added. These are indicated in the Notes by an asterisk. The Notes also provide the sources for the poems and may serve to acknowledge my debt to the several libraries, journals, and private collectors who have graciously made their holdings available for publication. I am most grateful to them for their kindness and to the many other persons who have aided me with this collection.

Nathaniel Hawthorne   Poems

The Charms of Sweet Music

The charms of sweet Music no pencil can paint.
They calm the rude Savage, enliven the saint,
Make sweeter our pleasures, more joyous our joy.
With raptures we feel, yet those raptures n'er cloy.

Moderate Views **W**ith passions unruffled, untainted by pride,
By reason my life let me square.
The wants of my nature are cheaply supplied,
And the rest are but folly and care.
How vainly through infinite trouble and strife,
The many their labours employ,
Since all that is truly delightful in life,
Is what all if they please may enjoy.

Lady Fair   *Lady fair, will you not listen*
To my ardent vows of love?
Love that in my eyes doth glisten,
And is firm as Heaven above.

Thomas *Then, oh Thomas, rest in glory!*
Hallowed be thy silent grave,—
Long thy name in Salem's story
Shall live, and honour o'er it wave.

Earthly Pomp

Oh, earthly pomp is but a dream,
And like a meteor's short-lived gleam;
And all the sons of glory soon
Will rest beneath the mould'ring stone.
And Genius is a star whose light
Is soon to sink in endless night,
And heavenly beauty's angel form
Will bend like flower in winter's storm.

I saw where in his lowly grave
Departed Genius lay.
And mournful yew trees o'er it wave,
To hide it from the day.

Oh do not bid me part from thee,
For I will leave thee never.
Although thou throw'st thy scorn on me,
Yet I will love forever.

There is no heart within my breast,
For it has flown away,
And till I knew it was thy guest,
I sought it night and day.

My Low and Humble Home *I left my low and humble home,*
Far from my Father's fields to roam.
My peaceful cot no more had charms,
My only joy was War's alarms.
I panted for the field of fight,
I gaz'd upon the deathless light,
Which o'er the Hero's grave is shed,
The glorious memory of the dead.
Ambition show'd a distant star,
That shed its radiance bright and far,
And pointed to a path which led
O'er heaps of dying and of dead;
Onward I press'd with eager feet,
And War's dread thunder still would greet
My reckless ears. Where'er I trod,
I saw the green and verdant sod,
Turn red with blood of slaughter'd foes,
And Fury veil'd in smoke arose.
I gain'd the envied height; and there,
I sigh'd for that lone cottage, where
The early hours of life flew by,
On wings of youthful ecstasy.
Too late I found that Glory's ray,
Could never bring one happy day.

Go to the Grave

Go to the grave where friends are laid,
And learn how quickly mortals fade,
Learn how the fairest flower must droop,
Learn how the strongest form must stoop,
Learn that we are but dust and clay,
The short-liv'd creatures of a day.
Yet do not sigh—there is a clime,
Where they will dwell through endless time,
Who here on earth their Maker serve,
And never from his precepts swerve.
The grave to them is but a road,
That leads them to that blest abode.

The Oak *I have seen the oak in its strength and pride,*
When its leaves were green, and boughs spread wide,
And a wild vine twin'd round its stately form,
And claim'd a shelter from the storm.
I have seen the oak when its beauty was gone,
And the wither'd trunk was left alone,
Yet still the wild vine twin'd luxuriant there,
And the oak e'en in age with its verdure was fair.

The Darken'd Veil

Oh could I raise the darken'd veil
Which hides my future life from me,
Could unborn ages slowly sail
Before my view—and could I see
My every action painted there,
To cast one look I would not dare.
There poverty and grief might stand,
And dark Despair's corroding hand,
Would make me seek the lonely tomb
To slumber in its endless gloom.
Then let me never cast a look,
Within Fate's fix'd mysterious book.

In Rapture Wild

Oh I have roam'd in rapture wild,
Where the majestic rocks are pil'd,
In lonely stern magnificence, around
The troubled Ocean's stedfast bound.
And I have seen the storms arise,
And darkness veil from mortal eyes,
The Heavens that shine so fair and bright
And all was solemn, silent night.
Then I have seen the Storm disperse
And Mercy hush the whirlwind fierce
And all my soul in transport own'd.
"There is a God, in Heaven enthron'd."

Days of my youth, ye fleet away,
As fades the bright Sun's cheering ray,
And scarce my infant hours are gone,
Ere Manhood's troubled step comes on.
My infant hours return no more
And all their happiness is o'er;
The stormy sea of life appears,
A scene of tumult and of tears.

Forms of Heroes

Ye Forms of Heroes slumb'ring here,
Beneath these tombstones cold and drear,
On which the moss of age has slept,
Since one fond heart has o'er you wept,
Oh tell me, if a Mortal's prayer,
Can ever wake your spirits, where
They sleep the dark dread sleep of death.
Tell me if now the laurel wreath,
Which Glory twin'd around your head,
Can wake amid the silent dead,
One glance of that proud martial blaze
Which led your feet in slaughter's ways.

Address to the Moon

*H*ow sweet the silver Moon's pale ray,
Falls trembling on the distant bay,
O'er which the breezes sigh no more,
Nor billows lash the sounding shore.
Say, do the eyes of those I love,
Behold thee as thou soar'st above,
Lonely, majestic and serene,
The calm and placid evening's Queen?
Say, if upon thy peaceful breast,
Departed spirits find their rest,
For who would wish a fairer home,
Than in that bright, refulgent dome?

The Billowy Ocean

The billowy Ocean rolls its wave,
Above the shipwreck'd Sailor's Grave,
Around him ever roars the Deep,
And lulls his wearied form to sleep,
Low in the deep Sea's darkest dell,
He hears no more the tempest swell.

The Dead
Their Vigil Keep
I

The moon is bright in that chamber fair,
And the trembling starlight enters there
With a soft and quiet gleam;
The wind sighs through the trees around,
And the leaves send forth a gentle sound,
Like the voices of a dream.

II *He has laid his weary limbs to sleep;*
But the dead around their vigil keep,
And the living may not rest.
There is a form on that chamber floor
Of beauty which should bloom no more,–
A fair, yet fearful guest!

III *The breath of morn has cooled his brow,*
And that shadowy form has vanished now,
Yet he lingers round the spot;
For the pale, cold beauty of that face,
And that form of more than earthly grace,
May be no more forgot.

IV *There is a grave by yon aged oak,*
But the moss-grown burial-stone is broke
That told how beauty faded;
But the sods are fresh o'er another head,
For the lover of that maiden dead
By the same tree is shaded.

17

The Ocean   *The Ocean has its silent caves,*
Deep, quite and alone;
Though there be fury on the waves,
Beneath them there is none.
The awful spirits of the deep
Hold their communion there;
And there are those for whom we weep,
The young, the bright, the fair.

Calmly the wearied seamen rest
Beneath their own blue sea.
The ocean solitudes are blest,
For there is purity.
The earth has guilt, the earth has care,
Unquiet are its graves;
But peaceful sleep is ever there,
Beneath the dark blue waves.

Moonlight   *We are beneath the dark blue sky,*
And the moon is shining bright.
Oh, what can lift the soul so high
  As the glow of a summer's night,
When all the gay are hush'd to sleep,
When they that mourn forget to weep,
  Beneath that gentle light?

Is there no holier, happier land
  Among those distant spheres,
Where we may meet that shadowy band,
  The dead of other years,
Where all the day the moonbeams rest,
And where at length the souls are blest
  Of those that dwell in tears?

Oh, if the happy ever leave
  Their bowers of bliss on high,
To cheer the hearts of those that grieve
  And wipe the tear drop dry,
It is when the moonlight sheds its ray,
More pure and beautiful than day,
  And earth is like the sky.

The wine is bright, the wine is bright;
*   And gay the drinkers be:*
Of all that drain the bowl to-night,
*   Most jollily drain we.*
Oh, could one search the weary earth,—
*   The earth from sea to sea,—*
He'd turn and mingle in our mirth;
*   For we're the merriest three.*

Yet there are cares, oh, heavy cares!
*   We know that they are nigh:*
When forth each lonely drinker fares,
*   Mark then his altered eye.*
Care comes upon us when the jest
*   And frantic laughter die;*
And care will watch the parting guest—
*   Oh late, then let us fly!*

A Jolly Drinker *I've been a jolly drinker this five and twenty year,*
And still a jolly drinker, my friends, you see me here:
I sing the joys of drinking; bear a chorus, every man,
With pint pot and quart pot and clattering of can.

The Downward Glance

*O*h, Man can seek the downward glance,
And each kind word—affection's spell—
Eye, voice, its value can enhance;
For eye may speak, and tongue can tell.

But Woman's love, it waits the while
To echo to another's tone,
To linger on another's smile,
Ere dare to answer with its own.

Walking on
the Sea

*A*nd when even was now come, his disciples went down unto the sea, and entered into a ship, and went over the sea toward Capernaum: and it was now dark, and Jesus was not come to them. And the sea arose, by reason of a great wind that blew. So when they had rowed about five and twenty or thirty furlongs, they see Jesus walking on the sea, and drawing nigh unto the ship; and they were afraid. But he saith unto them, "It is I; be not afraid." Then they willingly received him into the ship; and immediately the ship was at the land whither they went.–John vi. 16-21.

I *When the storm of the mountains on Galilee fell,*
      And lifted its waters on high;
   And the faithless disciples were bound in the spell
      Of mysterious alarm—their terrors to quell,
      Jesus whispered, "Fear not, it is I."

II *The storm could not bury that word in the wave,*
       For 'twas taught through the tempest to fly;
    It shall reach his disciples in every clime,
    And his voice shall be near in each troublous time,
       Saying, "Be not afraid, it is I."

III *When the spirit is broken with sickness or sorrow,*
        And comfort is ready to die;
     The darkness shall pass, and in gladness to-morrow
     The wounded complete consolation shall borrow
        From His life-giving word, "It is I."

23

IV When death is at hand, and the cottage of clay
    Is left with a tremulous sigh,
The gracious forerunner is smoothing the way
For its tenant to pass to unchangeable day,
    Saying, "Be not afraid, it is I."

V When the waters are passed, and the glories unknown
    Burst forth on the wondering eye,
The compassionate "Lamb in the midst of the throne"
Shall welcome, encourage, and comfort his own,
    And say, "Be not afraid, it is I."

The Star of
Calvary

*A*nd it was about the sixth hour, and there was a darkness over all the earth.—St. Luke xxiii. 44.

I   *It is the same infrequent star,—*
    The all-mysterious light,
That like a watcher, gazing on
    The changes of the night,
Toward the hill of Bethlem took
    Its solitary flight.

II   *It is the same infrequent star;*
    Its sameness startleth me:
Although the disc is red as blood,
    And downward, silently,
It looketh on another hill,—
    The hill of Calvary!

III   *Nor noon, nor night; for to the west*
    The heavy sun doth glow;
And, like a ship, the lazy mist
    Is sailing on below;
Between the broad sun and the earth
    It tacketh to and fro.

IV   *There is no living wind astir;*
    The bat's unholy wing
25   *Threads through the noiseless olive trees,*

Like some unquiet thing
Which playeth in the darkness, when
The leaves are whispering.

V Mount Calvary! Mount Calvary!
All sorrowfully still,
That mournful tread, it rends the heart
With an unwelcome thrill;
The mournful tread of them that crowd
Thy melancholy hill!

VI There is a cross, not one alone,
'Tis even three I count,
Like columns on the mossy marge
Of some old Grecian fount;
So pale they stand, so drearily,
On that mysterious Mount.

VII Behold, O Israel! behold,
It is no human One,
That ye have dared to crucify.
What evil hath he done?
It is your King, O Israel!
The God-begotten Son!

VIII A wreath of thorns, a wreath of thorns!
Why have ye crowned him so?

That brow is bathed in agony,
 'Tis veiled in every wo;
Ye saw not the immortal trace
 Of Deity below.

IX It is the foremost of the Three
 Resignedly they fall,
Those deathlike, drooping features,
 Unbending, blighted all:
The Man of Sorrows, how he bears
 The agonizing thrall!

X 'Tis fixed on thee, O Israel!
 His gaze!—how strange to brook;
But that there's mercy blended deep
 In each reproachful look,
'Twould search thee, till the very heart
 Its withered home forsook.

XI To God! to God! how eloquent
 The cry, as if it grew,
By those cold lips unuttered, yet
 All heartfelt rising through,—
"Father in heaven! forgive them, for
 They know not what they do!"

The Sage of
Apple Slump

There dwelt a Sage at Apple Slump
Whose dinner never made him plump;
Give him carrots, potatoes, squash, parsnips, and peas,
And some boiled macaroni without any cheese,
And a plate of raw apples to hold on his knees,
And a glass of sweet cider, to wash down all these;
And he'd prate of the Spirit as long as you'd please,
This airy Sage of Apple Slump!

There Was an
Old Boy

There was an old boy, with a new coat and breeches,
Who jumped over fences and tumbled in ditches,
While the mud and the mire spattered higher and higher,
Till he went to the fire, and, as he grew drier,
Burnt great holes in his new coat and breeches.

An Old Lady of   *There was an Old Lady of Guessme,*
    Guessme   *Whose talking did greatly distress me;*
    She talked of the nigger,
    And still she grew bigger,
    This tiresome Old Lady of Guessme!

A Young Man
Went to College

There was a young man went to college
Inflamed with a thirst after knowledge
But was hazed so severely
That he saw very clearly
That he'd better have not come to College.

Oh Snow That Comes When Violets Ought to Bloom

Oh snow that comes
When violets ought to bloom!
Oh thunderous drums
That lead men to the tomb!

Oh doleful robin,
Come from warmer climes!
Oh wretched bobbin',
Suiting alone my rhymes!
Oh heat that vainly strives
To dry up mud!
Oh myriad of young and happy lives,
Untimely quenched by rebel hands in blood.

So must the virtuous look
To higher spheres,
Although the little brook
Be swelled with tears!

Notes   *The Charms of Sweet Music**
MS: C. Waller Barrett Collection, Alderman Library, University
of Virginia. ca. 1815.

Moderate Views
MS: Essex Institute, Salem, Mass. Letter of 13 Feb. 1817.

*Lady Fair**
MS: Rare Books and Special Collections, University of California,
Berkeley. Elizabeth Hawthorne, letter of 20 Dec. 1865; ca.
1817.

*Thomas**
MS: Rare Books and Special Collections, University of California,
Berkeley. Elizabeth Hawthorne, letter of 20 Dec. 1865; ca.
1817.

*Earthly Pomp**
MS: Pierpont Morgan Library, New York City. Letter of 28 Sept.
1819.

*Where Genius Lay**
MS: Pierpont Morgan Library, New York City. Letter of 28 Sept.
1819.

*Do Not Bid Me Part**
MS: Pierpont Morgan Library, New York City. Letter of 28 Sept.
1819.

*My Low and Humble Home**
MS: Essex Institute, Salem, Mass. "The Spectator," 21 Aug. 1820.

*Go to the Grave**
MS: Essex Institute, Salem, Mass. "The Spectator," 28 Aug. 1820.

*The Oak**
MS: Essex Institute, Salem, Mass. "The Spectator," 28 Aug. 1820.

*The Darken'd Veil**
MS: Essex Institute, Salem, Mass. "The Spectator," 4 Sept. 1820.

*In Rapture Wild**
MS: Essex Institute, Salem, Mass. "The Spectator," 4 Sept. 1820.

*Days of My Youth**
MS: Essex Institute, Salem, Mass. "The Spectator," 11 Sept. 1820.

*Forms of Heroes**
MS: Essex Institute, Salem, Mass. "The Spectator," 11 Sept. 1820.

Address to the Moon
MS: Essex Institute, Salem, Mass. "The Spectator," 18 Sept. 1820.

*The Billowy Ocean**
MS: Essex Institute, Salem, Mass. "The Spectator," 25 Sept. 1820.

*The Dead Their Vigil Keep**
Printed: Julian Hawthorne, *Hawthorne and His Wife: A Biography* (Boston and New York, 1884), I, 102. ca. 1820.

The Ocean
Printed: Salem *Gazette*, XXXIX (26 Aug. 1825), 1.

Moonlight
Printed: *Independent Chronicle and Boston Patriot*, LXV (16 Aug. 1826), 4.

*The Wine is Bright**
Printed: Nathaniel Hawthorne, *Fanshawe*, Chapter V; ca. 1827-28.

*A Jolly Drinker**
Printed: Nathaniel Hawthorne, *Fanshawe*, Chapter V; ca. 1827-28.

*The Downward Glance**
Printed: Nathaniel Hawthorne, "The Threefold Destiny," *American Monthly Magazine*, V (Mar., 1838), 234.

Walking on the Sea
Printed: Rufus Griswold, ed., *Scenes in the Life of the Saviour by the Poets and Painters* (Philadelphia, 1845), pp. 95-96.

The Star of Calvary
Printed: Rufus Griswold, ed., *Scenes in the Life of the Saviour by the Poets and Painters* (Philadelphia, 1845), pp. 164-167.

*The Sage of Apple Slump**
MS: Henry E. Huntington Library, San Marino, Calif. (H.M. 1220). 1862.

*There Was an Old Boy**
MS: Pierpont Morgan Library, New York City. 1862.

*An Old Lady of Guessme**
Printed: Julian Hawthorne, *Hawthorne and His Wife: A Biography* (Boston and New York, 1884), II, 322. 1862.

*A Young Man Went to College**
34   MS: Henry E. Huntington Library, San Marino, Calif. ca. 1862.

Oh Snow That Comes When Violets Ought to Bloom
MS: Henry E. Huntington Library, San Marino, California; (H.M.
      11042). April, 1863. [Accompanied by Una Hawthorne's
      note: "Verse that Papa and I composed together for fun."]

Poems

was composed by The Composing Room, Inc.,
New York, New York, and was printed and bound
by Kingsport Press, Inc., Kingsport, Tennessee
in an edition of 750 copies.
The type is Palatino, designed by Hermann Zapf.
The end sheets are Tumba Ingres, supplied by
Andrews/Nelson/Whitehead, and the cover paper
is Curtis' Tweedweave.
The text paper is Mohawk's Superfine.
Designer: Edward G. Foss.
General Editor: Walker Cowen.